531.6
WHI   Whitehouse, Patty

        Pushes and pulls

DATE DUE

SE 15 08			
DE 22 08			
FE 2 '09			
OC 5 '09			
SE 19 '11			

Pushes And Pulls

Patty Whitehouse

Rourke
Publishing LLC
Vero Beach, Florida 32964

www.rourkepublishing.com

PHOTO CREDITS: © David and Patricia Armentrout: pages 4, 5, 6, 11, 13, 16, 20, 21; © PIR: pages 7, 10, 14, 18, 19; © constructionphotographs.com: pages 8, 9, 17; © Daniel Hyams: page 15; © Craig Lopetz: page 12

Editor: Robert Stengard-Olliges

Cover and interior design by Nicola Stratford

Library of Congress Cataloging-in-Publication Data

Whitehouse, Patricia, 1958-
  Pushes and pulls / Patty Whitehouse.
     p. cm. -- (Construction forces)
  Includes index.
  ISBN 1-60044-193-9 (hardcover)
  ISBN 1-59515-550-3 (softcover)
  1. Conveying machinery--Juvenile literature. 2. Force and
energy--Juvenile literature. 3. Building sites--Juvenile literature. I.
Title. II. Series: Whitehouse, Patricia, 1958- Construction forces.
  TJ1385.W48 2007
  531'.6--dc22
                           2006008862

Printed in the USA

CG/CG

Rourke Publishing

www.rourkepublishing.com – sales@rourkepublishing.com
Post Office Box 3328, Vero Beach, FL 32964
1-800-394-7055

Table of Contents

Construction Site

People and **machines** work here. It is a
construction site.

The people and machines use pushes and pulls to get work done.

Pushing and Pulling

Some workers push things when they work. This worker pushes snow out of the way.

Some workers pull things when they work. This worker pulls a **trowel** on concrete.

What is Force?

When something moves, it uses **force**. A force is a push or a pull.

Workers, **tools**, and trucks push and pull things.
They use force when they work.

Tools That Push

A shovel is a pushing tool. Workers push it under the dirt to get dirt out of the way.

A hammer is a pushing tool. It uses force to push the nail into the wood.

Machines That Push

Jackhammers move up and down very quickly. They push on concrete to break it up.

A construction stapler uses a lot of force. It pushes staples into wood.

Big Machines That Push

A bulldozer uses a **scoop**. It uses a lot of force to push a lot of dirt.

A wrecking ball is at the bottom of a cable. It uses a lot of force to push down the building.

Tools That Pull

One end of a hammer is a claw. It pulls nails out of wood.

Fish Tape

Electricians work with wire. They pull wires through the walls with a fish tape.

Machines That Pull

A pulley and steel cable on this crane can pull up heavy loads.

Air can make a strong pulling force. Air in the shop **vacuum** pulls dirt into the hose.

Big Machines That Pull

An excavator uses a big scoop. It pulls dirt out of the ground.

Hitch

The hitch is on the back of the truck. The truck pulls a trailer that hooks to the hitch.

Try It!

You can push and pull, too. Put a load in a wagon.
Use the handle to pull it. Or push the wagon in
the back.

GLOSSARY

construction site (kuhn STRUHKT shun SITE): a place where workers build

electrician (i lek TRISH uhn): worker whose job deals with electricity

force (FORSS): a push or a pull

machine (muh SHEEN): something that uses energy to help people work

scoop (SKOOP): the shovel part of a bulldozer or back hoe

tool (TOOL): something used to do work

trowel (TROU uhl): tool used to smooth concrete

vacuum (VAK yoom): machine that uses moving air to clean

INDEX

FURTHER READING

Kilby, Don. *At a Construction Site.* Kids Can Press, 2003.
Olson, K. C. *Construction Countdown.* Henry Holt, 2004.
Twist, Clint. *Force and Motion.* Bearport Publishing: New York: 2005

WEBSITES TO VISIT

http://www.bbc.co.uk/schools/scienceclips/ages/5_6/pushes_pulls.shtml
http://science.howstuffworks.com/engineering-channel.htm
http://www.bobthebuilder.com/usa/index.html

ABOUT THE AUTHOR

Patty Whitehouse has been a teacher for 17 years. She is currently a Lead Science teacher in Chicago, where she lives with her husband and two teenage children. She is the author of more than 100 books about science for children.